# I'd Rather be Grilling!

Graphic Design by Lee Ann Jack-Jesionowski
Editing by Lisa Minch

ISBN 0-9769375-0-6

Printed and bounded in the USA.

www.idratherbegrilling.com

# Acknowledgements

This cookbook is dedicated to all our friends and family

who have bragged about our cooking throughout the years and

to all our golfing buddies who continue to foster our love for the game.


Thanks also to our children, Dylan & Lauryn,

who show us unconditional love in their own special ways.


Love,

Clint & Michelle

# Table Of Contents

# F.Y.I.

t.  =  teaspoon

T.  =  tablespoon

 =  spicy

# Introduction

Whether you are a novice golfer and a grill master or vice versa,

we hope that you enjoy our most requested recipes from the grill.

We've picked our favorites and kept them simple

so that you have time to shoot an extra 9.


For most of these recipes, either a gas or charcoal grill will do.

But for special occasions, we recommend taking a few extra minutes

to fire up the coals to achieve the unmatched smoky flavor

of summertime grilling.

# Tee it up!

## – appetizers –

This recipe will impress your guests and disappear quickly!

# "Putt for dough" breadbowl

round loaf of sourdough bread
6 oz. Monterrey jack cheese, sliced
½ cup unsalted butter, melted
¼ cup sun-dried julienne cut tomatoes in oil (from jar)
1 clove garlic, minced
½ t. kosher salt

Slice bread in ½ inch checkerboard pattern,
to within 1 inch of the bottom of loaf.
(Do NOT cut all the way through).
Stuff thin slices of cheese in between openings of bread.
Combine melted butter, sun-dried tomatoes & minced garlic.
Pour mixture over bread. Sprinkle bread with kosher salt.
Use indirect heat to grill bread in bowl made of aluminum foil;
covered for first 20 minutes, uncovered for another 15 minutes,
or until cheese is bubbly.

**Serves 6**

Have lots of wet wipes and a cold beverage available
when eating these spicy wings.

# "Gimme" another buffalo wing

2 lb. bag frozen chicken wings & drummettes

<u>rub</u>
2 T. paprika
2 T. brown sugar
¼ t. black pepper

<u>sauce</u>
12 oz. bottle of Louisiana hot sauce
1 stick of butter, melted

Thaw wings.
Combine rub ingredients.
Place wings in a plastic bag and coat with rub.
Refrigerate wings for 2-3 hours.
Combine sauce ingredients in a deep bowl.
Grill wings over medium direct heat for 2 minutes per side.
Using BBQ tongs, individually dip wings in sauce and return to grill,
for an additional 25 minutes, or until cooked through.
While grilling, baste wings with sauce and flip often.

**Serves 6**

Once you try this recipe,
you'll never settle for fried calamari again.

# "Hole in one" calamari

2½ lbs. raw squid rings

rub
3 T. coarsely ground black pepper
4 t. lemon zest
1½ T. kosher salt

drizzle
juice of 2 lemons
1 cup olive oil
2 cloves garlic, minced
½ t. pepper

Combine rub ingredients in a small bowl. Rub into calamari.
Mix drizzle ingredients together and divide in half.
Brush grill skillet with small amount of olive oil.
Grill calamari in skillet for 4 minutes or until cooked through over direct heat.
Turn occasionally to avoid over cooking.
Use half the drizzle to baste calamari while grilling.
Place cooked calamari in a large serving bowl and pour remaining drizzle on top.
Squeeze a wedge of lemon on top just before serving.

**Serves 6**

Natural peanut butter works best with this satay.

# "Chip in" spicy satay

1 lb. boneless, skinless chicken breast, cut in 1 inch chunks
1 cup Italian salad dressing

peanut sauce
¼ cup chunky peanut butter
¼ cup soy sauce
¼ cup + 2 T. vegetable oil
2 cloves garlic, minced
1 t. crushed red pepper
½ t. ground ginger

Place chicken and salad dressing in a plastic ziploc bag.
Marinate in refrigerator for 6-8 hours.
Thread chicken chunks on small 6 inch metal skewers.
Discard marinade.
Combine peanut sauce ingredients in a microwave safe shallow bowl.
Grill chicken, turning often for 5-6 minutes over direct heat, until cooked through.
Warm peanut sauce in microwave just before serving.
Dip skewers in warm sauce.

**Serves 4**

# In the Fairway

## – main "course" –

Boneless chicken thighs are available at Sam's Club.

# Clint's "famous" boneless chicken thighs

8-10 boneless chicken thighs
1½ T. kosher salt
1 cup Zesty Italian salad dressing
½ t. freshly ground black pepper

Rub salt into chicken thighs.
Place chicken in a large plastic ziploc bag.
Pour salad dressing over chicken & sprinkle with black pepper.
Seal bag and rub outside of bag to thoroughly coat thighs.
Marinate in refrigerator overnight.
Discard marinade.
Grill chicken over high heat for 5 minutes on one side.
Flip chicken and grill another 4-5 minutes or until cooked through.

**Serves 4**

Serve with "Closest to the pin" veggie skewers.

# What a "shank" steak

1½ lbs. flank steak

marinade
¼ cup Southern Comfort
  (or favorite whiskey)
2 T. soy sauce

spicy rub
1 T. paprika
1 T. brown sugar
1 t. chili power
1 t. ground black pepper
1 t. garlic salt
½ t. cayenne pepper

Place steak and marinade ingredients in ziploc bag.
Marinate in refrigerator for 24 hours.
Discard marinade.
Combine ingredients for spicy rub.
Rub mixture into steak.
Let stand 20 minutes while preparing grill.
Grill over medium heat for 7 minutes on each side
or until desired doneness.
Cut steak diagonally across the grain into thin slices.
Serve with creamy horseradish or Dijon mustard.

**Serves 4**

These burgers deliver a burst of flavor with every bite.

# "Par 5" juicy blue cheese burgers

1½ lbs. ground beef
4 oz. crumbled blue cheese
2 T. coarsley ground black pepper
2 t. Lawry's seasoned salt
1½ t. garlic powder

Sprinkle ground beef with black pepper, seasoned salt, and garlic powder.
Mix well.
Divide seasoned ground beef into 6 patties.
Using about half the container of blue cheese,
stuff approximately 1 T. of blue cheese into the center of each burger and pack tightly.
Save the remaining blue cheese for the tops of the burgers.

Grill over medium heat for 4-5 minutes per side.
Sprinkle burgers with remaining blue cheese just before removing from the grill.

**Serves 6**

This dish is messy but delicious!

# "FORE!" peppery shrimp

2 lbs. frozen jumbo cooked shrimp
4 limes
1 cup butter, melted
4 T. worchestershire sauce
2 T. ground black pepper
2 cloves garlic, minced
½ t. Old Bay seasoning
½ t. salt

loaf of crusty French bread, sliced

Thaw shrimp.
Combine the juice of 2 limes and the next 6 ingredients in a disposable aluminum pan.
Slice other 2 limes.
Add shrimp and lime slices to the pan.
Pour butter mixture over shrimp, coating thoroughly.
Grill shrimp in pan over indirect high heat for 8-10 minutes, stirring occasionally, until hot.
Dip slices of bread in remaining sauce.

**Serves 4**

Even a "non-eggplant eater" will enjoy these tasty sandwiches.

# "Golfer's paradise" eggplant sandwiches

2 medium-sized eggplants
2 T. kosher salt
¼ cup vegetable oil

spicy drizzle
¾ cup olive oil
3 T. balsamic vinegar
5 cloves garlic, minced
1 T. dried parsley
1 t. crushed red pepper

1 round loaf of **Hawaiian** bread

Slice eggplant to ¼ inch thickness.
Place eggplant slices on a cutting board.
Sweat eggplant by generously sprinkling slices with kosher salt on both sides.
Let stand about 20 minutes. Rinse eggplant with cool water and pat dry.
Liberally coat eggplant slices with vegetable oil.
Mix drizzle ingredients.
Grill eggplant 8-10 minutes until tender, turning occasionally.
Transfer to a plate. Top eggplant with the spicy drizzle.
Slice bread to ½ inch thickness.
Make sandwiches using 2-3 slices of eggplant per sandwich.

**Serves 4**

These chops go well with the "Out of bounds" corn on the cob.

# "Slow fade" savory lamb chops

2 lbs. lamb chops

marinade
1/2 cup stone ground mustard
4 T. dry sherry
2 T. balsamic vinegar
2 T. brown sugar
4 green onions, sliced
5 cloves garlic, minced
1 t. dried rosemary, crushed
1/2 t. salt
1/4 t. crushed red pepper

Combine marinade ingredients in a small bowl.
Place lamb chops in a large ziploc plastic bag.
Cover chops with marinade and rub chops to thoroughly coat.
Marinate in refrigerator for 24 hours. Discard marinade.
Grill chops over direct heat 6 minutes per side for rare,
8-9 minutes per side for medium doneness.

**Serves 6**

This recipe is **ONLY** recommended for a charcoal grill/smoker.

# Smokin' "birdie"

| | |
|---|---|
| 6 pound turkey breast | **marinade** |
| | 2 cups brown sugar |
| | $\frac{3}{4}$ cup salt |
| | 2 bay leaves |
| mesquite wood chips | 4 cloves garlic, minced |
| | 2 T. black peppercorns |
| | 3 cups very warm water |

Place first 5 marinade ingredients in a large container.
Pour warm water over ingredients to dissolve. Add turkey breast.
Marinate overnight, turning occasionally.
To achieve an extra smoky flavor,
soak a handful of wood chips in 2 cups of water over night in a disposable container.
Remove turkey from container and discard marinade.
Rinse turkey breast with cool water for a couple minutes.
Once charcoal turns gray, add several wood chips to the coals.
Grill turkey over indirect heat for $2\frac{1}{2}$ - $3\frac{1}{2}$ hours or until thoroughly cooked,
adding more wood chips as necessary.

**Serves 10**

Serve with A "slice" of smoky yams.

# "Drive for show" parmesan pork chops

4 pork chops, 1½ inch thick
2 T. Liquid Smoke

rub
2 t. kosher salt
2 t. parmesan cheese
2 t. paprika
1 t. ground black pepper
1 t. crushed red pepper

¼ cup parmesan cheese

Butterfly chops.
Place chops in a bowl and top with Liquid Smoke.
Combine 5 rub ingredients in a small bowl.
Rub into chops. Set aside for 10 minutes.
Grill over direct heat approximately 4 minutes per side.
Sprinkle chops with parmesan cheese,
before removing from grill.

**Serves 4**

# In the Rough

## - grilled veggies -

Make sure you're "closest to the grill" to get one.

# "Closest to the pin" veggie skewers

2 green zucchini
1 yellow zucchini squash
4 oz. whole mushrooms
1 red bell pepper
1 green bell pepper
1 red onion

marinade
½ cup of olive oil
1 t. thyme
1 t. oregano
¼ t. black ground pepper
⅛ t. kosher salt

Wash all vegetables.
Cut the zucchini, peppers and onion into 1 inch chunks.
Combine marinade ingredients.
Marinate vegetables for 1-2 hours.
Thread all vegetables onto metal skewers.
Grill for 8-10 minutes turning often, basting with marinade.

**Serves 4**

For grilling purists, skip the microwave directions.
Prick, wrap and grill whole potatoes for 45 minutes to 1 hour.

# A "slice" of smoky yams

2 large sweet potatoes
½ stick of butter
½ cup brown sugar
2 t. cinnamon

Wash potatoes and prick skin with a fork.
Place potatoes in a microwave safe casserole dish
with ½ cup water.
Microwave potatoes for 10-13 minutes.
While potatoes are still hot, carefully peel and slice.
Place in a bowl made of aluminum foil.
Top with pats of butter, cinnamon and brown sugar.
Grill for 10-15 min.

**Serves 4**

For the best possible flavor,
try to buy or better yet pick your corn on the day you're making it.

# "Out of bounds" corn on the cob

6 fresh ears of corn

butter sauce
2 sticks butter, melted
2 cloves garlic, minced
1 T. dried rosemary
1 t. salt
1 t. dried parsley
½ t. ground black pepper

Shuck and wash corn.
Combine ingredients for butter sauce.
Pour mixture in a big shallow bowl.
Dip corn in butter sauce.
Wrap each ear of corn in aluminum foil.
Grill over direct heat for 15-20 minutes, or until tender.
Turn often.
Carefully unwrap corn.
Serve with remaining butter sauce for dipping.

**Serves 6**

# On the Green

## - desserts -

YUMMY!

# "Sweet spot" feelin' no pain bananas

4 bananas, peeled & sliced
½ cup brown sugar
½ cup coconut rum
¼ cup butter
1 T. ground cinnamon

Put banana slices into a foil oven bag.
Add brown sugar, coconut rum, and slices of butter.
Sprinkle with ground cinnamon.
Close the bag and grill over low heat for 25 minutes,
basting bananas occasionally until tender and golden.
Serve over French vanilla ice cream.

**Serves 4**

Also goes well with cinnamon ice cream.

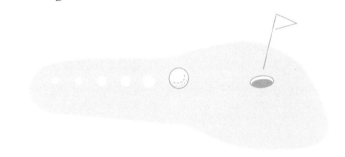

# Nothin' but "fairway" fruit crisp

2 medium Granny Smith apples, peeled & thinly sliced
2 pears, peeled & sliced
2 T. sugar

topping
2 packets apple cinnamon instant oatmeal
¼ cup flour
¼ cup brown sugar
5 T. butter, softened
½ t. nutmeg
8 oz. container Cool Whip

Place fruit in a disposable aluminum pan.
Sprinkle with sugar.
Combine topping ingredients and crumble over fruit.
Grill over medium heat for 20 minutes, or until golden and bubbly.
Top each serving with a spoonful of Cool Whip.

**Serve 6**

Best enjoyed around a camp fire while singing Kumbaya.

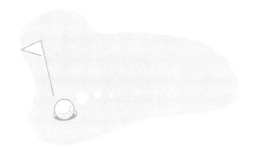

# "Double eagle" chocolate cinnamon s'mores

6 whole cinnamon graham crackers
12 marshmallows
1.55 oz. Hershey milk chocolate bar
1.55 oz. Hershey special dark chocolate bar

Place 6 graham cracker halves on a two-ply sheet of aluminum foil.
Place 2 squares of both types of chocolate and 2 marshmallows
on each graham cracker half.
Cover with remaining graham cracker halves.

Wrap with another sheet of foil and grill over indirect heat for 2-3 minutes,
or until marshmallows melt.

**Serves 6**

# At the Clubhouse

## - summer drinks -

This potent pitcher is best prepared before your guests arrive;
so that the melting ice has a chance to dilute the alcohol a bit.

# Michelle's "mulligan" margaritas

12 oz. can frozen limeade concentrate
12 oz. bottle light beer
12 oz. Jose Cuervo light tequila
juice of 2 limes
1-2 drops green food coloring (optional)
4 cups ice cubes
2 limes for garnish
Grand Marnier


Blend limeade, beer, tequila and lime juice.
Pour mixture into a large pitcher.
Stir in food coloring.
Add ice.
Refrigerate for 1-2 hours.
Serve each margarita on the rocks with a slice of lime,
in a salted glass and a "free shot" of Grand Marnier.

ENJOY!

**Serve 6**

Make a pitcher before you tee off on a hot summer day!

# "19th hole" sangria

1.5 liter bottle Cabernet Sauvignon
½ cup brandy
¼ cup triple sec
1 cup orange juice
1 cup lemon juice
1 cup sugar
5 strawberries, sliced
10 grapes, cut in half
1 orange, sliced
1 lemon, sliced

2 cups sparkling water

Combine first 10 ingredients in a large pitcher and refrigerate 6 hours or more.
Add sparkling water,
serve over a tall glass of ice and enjoy!

**Serves 6**

Corona

Bud Light

Miller Genuine Draft

Guiness

Samuel Adams

(any one will do)

# Every golfer's "favorite" beer

On the 18th hole,
start off with a 300 yard drive straight down the fairway.
Using a 3 iron, nail your approach shot within 2 feet of the green.
Chip your ball right into the cup.
Proceed straight to the clubhouse.
Order your favorite icy cold beer.
Guzzle it down, basking in your glory.

**Serves 1 (you)**

# Index

A "slice" of smoky sweet yams, 41

## appetizers
"Chip-in" spicy satay, 17

"Gimme" another buffalo wing, 13

"Hole in one" calamari, 15

"Putt for dough" breadbowl, 11

## beef
"Par 5" juicy blue cheese burgers, 25

What a "shank" steak, 23

"Chip-in" spicy satay, 17

Clint's "famous" boneless chicken thighs, 21

"Closest to the pin" veggie skewers, 39

## desserts
"Double eagle" chocolate cinnamon s'mores, 51

Nothin' but "fairway" fruit crisp, 49

"Sweet spot" feelin' no pain bananas, 47

"Double eagle" chocolate cinnamon s'mores, 51

## drinks
"19th hole" sangria, 57

Every golfer's "favorite" beer, 59

Michelle's "mulligan" margaritas, 55

"Drive for show" parmesan pork chops, 35

Every golfer's "favorite" beer, 59

## fruit
Nothin' but "fairway" fruit crisp, 49

"Sweet spot" feelin' no pain bananas, 47

"FORE!" peppery shrimp, 27

"Gimme" another buffalo wing, 13

"Golfer's Paradise" eggplant sandwiches, 29

"Hole in one" calamari, 15